# VOICE : Social as it should be.

*The next generation social media*

# Table of Contents

# Chapter 1- Introduction

The popularity of social media platforms has been on the rise, getting big and bigger every day. Nearly every individual has one or two social media profiles that they use to interact with their colleagues, friends and acquaintances. Research has shown that most teenagers spend up to 9 hours each day on social media interacting with family and friends. Of course, this is made possible by use of tablets and smartphones.

However, a number of issues have been raised with the surging use of social media platforms. The biggest concern is with the management of user data. Most social media platforms have not been designed to meet the demands of their users, but to meet the needs of their stockholders. To solve this problem, Block.one invented Voice, a social media application that runs on the blockchain. Voice has been designed and developed with the user in mind. It is a very transparent social media platform where good quality content is used to sustain the community instead of using it for corporate purposes.

The launch of Voice was announced by Brendan Blumer, the CEO of Block.one, at the company's event held on June 1 at DC Armory in Washington, D.C. Your personal data and the content you post on your social media account is very valuable. With the current social media platforms, the business model has been designed such that only the platform reaps reward from these valuable things, not you. They auction your information to advertisers, flood your feed with ads that are dictated by the highest bidder, and pocket the profits. Voice is changing that!

Most social media platforms rely on bots and fake accounts for the creation, discovery, sharing and promotion of content. Voice will change this so that it is done by real users. It relies on an economy of ideas capable of sustaining itself so as to ensure that users benefit directly from their content and time they spend on the platform.

Voice will be running on the EOS public blockchain. To enhance transparency on Voice, the interactions will be done publicly. All users, including the user, the contributor and the platform will be governed by the same rules. There will be no invisible interests and hidden algorithms.

Block.one has introduced a unique and smart way to revolutionize social media. The EOS public blockchain on which it runs relies on the EOS.IO protocol, which has a very high speed and is good for free apps. Owing to the scalability, the users of the platform will have a smooth experience. EOSIO was developed to be used for creating a scalable, flexible and more secure blockchain framework to rebuild trust on the systems used today by enterprises and regular users. Due to this, networks built on EOSIO are highly used all in public blockchain platforms globally, making up to 70% of all blockchain activity.

The next version of the EOSIO protocol, the EOSIO Version 2, is expected to introduce a set of new features. EOS Version 2 will use EOS-VM, a WebAssembly Engine good for use in blockchain smart contracts. The users will be able to process smart contracts 12 times faster. The protocol will also be capable of using the web authentication standard provided by WebAuthn, meaning that applications running on the EOSIO platform will have a great security and usability. Such features and updates are in line with the goal of Block.one of adopting the use of blockchain technology in applications developed for use in enterprises and everyday life.

Block.one is prioritizing privacy, security and ease-of-use in all its projects, including Voice. To enhance the security of applications, Block.one is adopting the use of hardware security keys. This means that you will not have a problem with the security of your Voice account.

# Chapter 2- Mainstream Social Media situation

### Mainstream Social Media Intro

With the increasing demand for online communications and interactions, many social media

platforms have been developed. This has seen the following social media platforms rise to the

top:

### Facebook

Today, Facebook is the largest social media platform in the world with more than 2 billion users

and about 2.41 million monthly active users. It is also the social media platform with the most

diverse audience since you can find users of all ages on Facebook. However, a recent study

showed that the largest Facebook user base is made up of individuals aged between 25 to 34

years. That is why Facebook has become a great tool for marketing to individuals who are above

18 years old. Facebook also has a good gender balance, making a good platform for marketing to both males and females.


## YouTube

YouTube was acquired by Google by Google in 2006 after its launch in 2005. Today, it is the second largest search engine in the world after Google. Today, YouTube has above 1.9 billion subscribers. These users spend a billion hours watching YouTube videos every day, generating many views. This has made YouTube an excellent channel for individuals to reach and engage their consumers by creating compelling videos.

Statistics indicate that most YouTube users are aged between 18 and 49 years. The male users dominate the platform, accounting for 55% of all users and the remaining 45% of the total subscribers is made of female users. 74% of YouTube users watch brand channels each week. This has given companies an opportunity to reach active and interested audience consistently.

## Instagram

Instagram is owned by Facebook and it currently has more than 1 billion users. These users log into their Instagram accounts to enjoy the video and photo posts of their friends, family and even brands. Instagram promotes graphical content, which has made it a great social media platform for growing brands. A research done by Ad Espresso, 80% of Instagram users follow brands.

The platform is dominated by female users at 39% and male users at 30%, which explains why marketers use it to market brands consumed by females. Majority of these users are young people aged between 18 and 29 years, making 53% of the total Instagram users. This has made the platform the best social media channel to market brands consumed by individuals aged below 30 years.

## WeChat

WeChat began as a messaging app, just like Messenger and WhatsApp, later becoming an all-in-one platform. The platform can be used for messaging, calling, shopping online and making offline payments, making reservations, money transfer, booking taxis etc. Currently, WeChat has 1.06 billion users.

## Tumblr

Tumblr is a social networking and micro-blogging website launched by David Carp in 2007. Most people see it as a blogging platform rather than a social media platform. Currently, it has above 1 billion users and 371 million users visit it each month. 46% of Tumblr users are aged between 18 and 34 years. 52% of Tumblr user are male and 485 are female. Such a user base has given marketers a good platform for them to grow their brand.

## TikTok

This social media platform allows its users to create short videos with filters, music and other features. The videos can run for up to 60 seconds. In 2018, the app was downloaded 660M times, beating Facebook, Instagram and other social media apps. It is used by more than 500 million people every month. 66% of its users are aged below 30 years. On average, each user spends 52 minutes on the app per day, with 29% of all users opening TikTok each day.

## Weibo

Weibo, commonly known as Sia Weibo, is the Twitter for Chinese users since the use of Twitter is banned in China. Its users are able to get features similar to those of Twitter, including microblogging, commenting, uploading of videos and photos and accounts verification. The platform gets an average of 462 million users each month. 40% of Weibo users are aged between 23 and 30 years. The platform is dominated by male users, accounting for 57% of the total users, while women make 43%. In 2018, a 50% increase in livestreaming sessions was witnessed on the platform.

**Google+**

Google plus was founded by Google in 2011 to add a social layer on all Google products. However, the purpose of the platform has changed tremendously and numerous features have been added to it. Currently, Google+ has approximately 395 million active monthly users and more than 2 billion users from all over the world. 28% of these users are aged from 15 to 34 years. 55% of the total Google plus users comes from the United States. The platform is dominated by male users, accounting for 73.7% of the total Google plus users, while females account for only 26.3%.

**Reddit**

Reddit is a discussion forum and a website for rating web content. It was founded by Steve Huffman and Alexis Ohanian in 2005. Reddit has not much been publicized through the press, but it is gaining a vibrant and thriving community of people. Currently, the platform gets approximately 330 million active users every moth. Reddit also receives about 14 billion views every month. Each Reddit user spends approximately 13 minutes each day. Above 138,000 active communities have so far joined Reddit.

**Twitter**

Twitter has more than 330 million active monthly users, and it has become the best social media platform for one to receive trends and latest news on various topics of interest. Due to this, many marketers have used the platform to target users who may be interested in their brands. It is an excellent channel for sharing any updates made on existing brands and taking part in online communications that surround your industry.

Research has shown that 24% of men and 21% of women are on Twitter. This has made the platform a good channel for marketing brands for both males and females. The platform users tend to be young, with 36% of the users being aged between 18 and 29 years. However, users of older age groups also form a significant part of the Twitter membership.

**Problem 1: Personal Information**
Social media platforms depend on the users giving out their data. When you give out your data to a social media platform, they use it to communicate, analyze markets and build business models. This means that data is the food of social media.

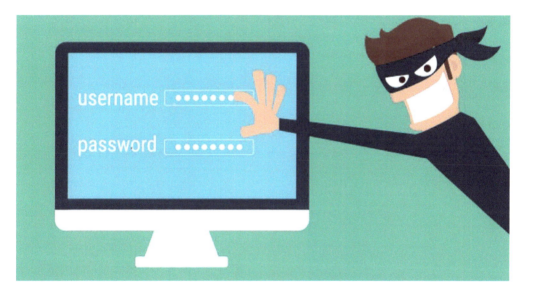

However, this data is your personal data, data that represents your digital self. Much of the data is very personal, like your name, email address, phone number etc. Other data such as your geo-location, online excursions, likes and dislikes is less personal, but it gives useful insights to the social media platforms. This data is not useful to the social media business models only, but also to insurance companies, cybercriminals and others who may want to use our personal information to tailor our views and know our supposed needs.

Since social media platforms rely on our data, they can impact our lives in a variety of different ways. Consider the case of Schrems vs. Facebook. Schrems accused Facebook of illegally transferring personal data from Europe to NSA (National Security Agency) in the United States. This was a violation of the European data protection law, which requires that a defined criteria be followed before personal data may be transferred outside the European Union. A Canadian citizen filed a dispute in court against Facebook for using her photo to run a sponsored campaign without her consent. The campaign had allowed the marketers to use the profile photo of any user who had clicked the like button on an advertising post. Just recently, Facebook has been accused of influencing the U.S presidential election through the UK based firm, Cambridge Analytica. That is what the personal data you provide on social media platforms can do!

Nowadays, hackers are looking for potential victims online. They use shortened URLS (Uniform Resource Locator) to trick users into visiting harmful sites. They also inject viruses and malware into their phones and computers. Hackers also install spyware programs into your laptop or mobile phone which can give them the details of the passwords you use on social media sites and other online platforms. They have realized that it is easy for them to spread malware, viruses and scams through social media than using traditional mechanisms like email addresses. It is very likely that you can easily trust messages you receive from your social media friends and followers.

Providing your personal information to a social media site makes you vulnerable to identity thieves. They target social information data such your email address and date of birth. Once they get email address, they can proceed to hack it. Once they gain access to your email, they can click the "forgot password" option on Facebook and reset your Facebook account password. They will then be able to access all the information you have added on your Facebook account.

Most social media sites have developed mobile apps with location based services, allowing users to check in their current location. This means that the location of the user will be exposed to all individuals the user is located to on that social media platform. Malicious individuals can use such information to know your location and track your movements. Again, when you tell people where you are going, thieves and burglars may target your home or business. For instance, if you say that you have gone for a long vacation in London, thieves will know how long you will stay over there. This will give them enough time to plan their ill motives.

Majority of social media users use smartphones. Social media platforms are taking advantage of mobile devices, especially their location based services. This has increased the security threat of users. Most smartphones collect the location information of their users without the users' knowledge. Social media apps are greatest beneficiaries of this information. Since there are no proper laws and legislations governing the use of such data, social media platforms are using the data for their own benefit without the consent of the users.

Many are the times most websites have asked you to turn over to your various social media accounts. A good example is when you want to login into a particular website. Nowadays, they are allowing users to login using their social media accounts. Many are the times employers request their employees to grant them access to their social media accounts to ensure that they don't share trade secrets or any confidential information. This makes the employees vulnerable to privacy violations.

Sharing your personal information on social media platforms makes you vulnerable to stalking and harassment. All social media privacy threats don't come only from strangers. Sometimes, it happens that the people who were your close friends turn out to be less friendly. Social media have made it easy for such people to stalk ad cyberbully you.

I recently encountered a case where a lady broke up with her boyfriend. The two were in campus. The man knew the password of the Facebook account password of the lady. The lady was shocked when her friends contacted her and asked her about the pornographic content she was posting on her Facebook account. She realized that the man had changed her Facebook account password. This continued for a while and by the time it stopped, most of her friends, acquaintances and even relatives had read the content.

When you post something on your social media account, you may think that it will only be accessed by your friends. However, the platforms allow your friends to share content from their friends. Their friends will also be allowed to share the content and this circle continues.

Facebook offers a feature called *closed groups*. Recently, there was an uproar about these groups. There are special groups for individuals with health issues as well as addicts. Users with such issues use those groups to share different kinds of information, meaning that such groups can have information which is very sensitive. Users in such groups also expect to be anonymized. However, an investigation done by Sky News found that the groups can be searched with much ease and the membership list is readily available. This means that information shared in such groups can easily be exposed. Insurance companies and potential employers can access such groups to collect personal information. This may also lead to identity theft.

**Problem 2: Advertisement**
Social media platforms are using your personal information to push products to you. Nowadays, video ads have become the norm of social media platforms. When you try to watch a video on Facebook, you will have to pause for some seconds to wait for an ad to run. They are not even providing you with an option for you to skip the ad. Video ads have also become the norm of

YouTube. Before you can watch your YouTube video, you may have to wait for some seconds for the ad to run. Even though they provide a way for you to skip the ad, this comes after some seconds have elapsed. Some YouTube video ads run for minutes.

Your location data, such as the shopping malls you visit is a prime data for digital marketers. When they combine it with your personal data, they will successfully push products to you. This is very irritating, and what irritates most is the use of artificial intelligence by marketing industries on the personal information obtained from social media profiles. A combination of social media, artificial intelligence and marketing have given marketers a perfect combination to advertise their brands. The work of marketers becomes effective when there is personalization, and artificial intelligence has made this a reality. For example, by use of artificial intelligence tools, a marketer is able to tell the days when a user uses his or her social media accounts and the exact times when the user is online. When this is combined with other demographic information such as age, location and social media usage, the marketer can push more focused ads to the user.

It is obvious that marketing ads on social media platforms are disturbing. Most social media platform pages are filled with ads on all sides which distract the attention of the user. Most users are not even interested in the ads that are sent to them. That is why consumers are pushing against social media ads. Both the social media platforms and marketers should note that the more they push ads to consumers, the more they will push against it.

Ads have transformed the information economy from monetary payments to personal data bartering. The ad revolution is powered by the ability to accurately target ads to only the pinpoint demographics that the adviser has interest in reaching. The only laws governing the use of ads on social media dictate the type of audiences that should be targeted, with the factors under consideration being gender, race and age ranges. The social media platforms don't have measures to ensure that these are adhered to, but this has been left to the hands of the advertisers. Social media users are still asking, who should be held responsible for the illegal ads running on social media?

The social media advertising economy is done by targeting the user interests and demographics. On Facebook for example, if an advertiser wants to advertise its apartment building, he can request Facebook not to show the ad to minorities such as individuals with disabilities. If it is a job ad, the advertiser can request that the ad is not shown to women or to individuals of a particular age. The social media platforms allow such discriminatory ads to be run while benefitting from the users.

The advertisers argue that their goal is to maximize returns on their advertising investment by targeting social media users whose demographics match their products. Yes, they target individuals who most often purchase their products. The argument is that there is no need to waste money marketing to individuals who have not shown interest in the product. Such mindset has a problem in that it reinforces stereotypes and encourages discrimination. In the U.S for example, this is illegal.

The platforms have argued that before the digital era, it was possible to run ads on various print and broadcast outlets and certain shows in a particular city with the goal of targeting their differing demographics and this was completely legal. Facebook has argued that targeting different age groups when running ads is not discriminatory, similarly to running job ads on TV shows and magazines targeted at older or younger people.

This argument has a problem in that the digital ad will be seen only by the targeted individuals, but anyone reading the newspaper or watching the show will see the ad. In short, if it is a carpentry job placed in a magazine, men may be targeted, but women will also see the ad. Even though the advertiser targets men, even women who are interested in carpentry will see the ad.

In contrast to this, if a social media ad is targeted to men only, women may never see the ad, even if they have all the qualifications required for the job. Some social media platforms such as Facebook provide an option for individuals to view the ads for a particular brand's Page regardless of the demographics the ad was targeted to. This means that in our previous example, the woman can visit the company's page and browse through all their ads to look for any job suitable to them. However, this is burdensome to her and gives men advantage over her. Men will be able to apply the job in time unlike women. Women may also never know that the company is hiring, meaning that they will miss on important opportunities that are available in the market. This shows that there is a great problem with the current social media ads.

# Chapter 3- EOS

**Introducing EOS**

Many non-specialists fail to understand some critical areas in the field of blockchain technology and cryptocurrency due to the use of technical terms. However, you don't have to worry as these will be made easy in this chapter.

Anybody with interest in cryptocurrency should understand the EOS technology. It is one of the latest technologies behind cryptocurrencies, and most probably, the most advanced one.

EOS is simply a decentralized platform designed to support the development of decentralized applications. A decentralized application is a type of application capable of handling a massive number of users simultaneously, rapidly and free of charge. EOS was developed by Dan Larimer.

## Why was EOS Developed?

The goal of EOS is to introduce a transparent and secure system that can be used to manage both local and global monetary transactions, providing its users with an alternative to the current banking system.

EOS has also introduced an appropriate system for running elections and referendums since the blockchain technology can be used to ensure that there is credibility and protect the election from rigging and fraud. EOS is also aimed at creating a global digital identity that individuals will use to travel across countries and own different properties. EOS was developed to overcome the weaknesses associated with Ethereum, meaning that the two are closely related.

After its launch, its cryptocurrency, EOSIO managed to appear in the top 10 cryptocurrencies within a very short period of time. The main function of Eos is to provide tools that are easy to use for the development of decentralized applications (dApps) and provide a system with which transactions can be accomplished immediately. Eos has also addressed the issue of scalability.

Here are the two main features of EOS that have made it disrupt the market:

- EOS does not charge any fee for transactions.

- It has introduced a technology that is capable of handling millions of transactions in a second.

EOS has also introduced readable account names, making it possible for the users to send tokens to a wallet address without having to copy the address. This is because these addresses are easy to read and save unlike in other cryptocurrencies.

**Advantages of EOS Blockchain**

## Get Started with EOSIO

The following are the advantages associated with the EOS blockchain:

1. It provides its users with the ability to create smart contracts using any WebAssembly-based programming language. Examples of such programming languages include JavaScript, Python, Go, .NET and others.

2. It supports parallel processing. This feature makes it possible for EOS to complete transactions quickly. There is no other cryptocurrency that provides this feature. EOS also provides its users with a limitless scalability expansion.

3. EOS supports multithreading. The multithreading was discovered in the 1990s. Despite this, no cryptocurrency platform has implemented this feature. However, EOS is

currently is developing this technology and it will be implemented on their platform very soon.

You may ask yourself, why has there been a delay in the implementation of this multi-threaded parallel processing? The reason is because careful and detailed work is needed to develop the cores of the system. First, there is a need to increase the number of transactions that can be handled by a single core as much as possible before proceeding to develop the multiple cores. Even though this feature needs to be completed as soon as possible, there is no blockchain technology that exceeded EOS in terms of speed so far.

4. EOS has low latency. Efforts are still undergoing to help reduce this latency further and allow the decentralized applications (dApps) to run smoothly.

5. On EOS, all users are given equal voting rights. Due to this, EOS has implemented the ideal concept of decentralized operating system. This has been made possible by use of the Delegated Proof of Stake consensus algorithm. With this algorithm, each user is allowed to vote for any critical decisions, meaning that all users take part in the decision making process. This is not the case with the other blockchain implementations that use the Proof of Stake (POS) and Proof of Work (POW) consensus algorithms, in which voting rights are given only to those with a greater stake or mining power.

The Delegated Proof of Stake is a new consensus algorithm that has been developed by Daniel Larimar.

6. Free transactions. EOS allows developers to run their applications on the EOS blockchain by use of staked EOS. The good news regarding the use of used resources to build applications is that the EOS token used for building the applications will not be spent. The developer will only be required to proof ownership of the token and they will be

allowed to use the EOS resources. Additionally, the application developers will be allowed to exchange the EOS network resources between each other.

7. EOS is self-sufficient and sustainable. Currently, a 5% inflation has been provided and is normally expended when it comes to continuous network development. This is not the case with other blockchain implementations since they don't have a generous, sustainable and equitable system that guarantees developers of a continuous funding of its development forever. Most blockchains have experiences disputes related to development and expenses.

**How are Blocks Produced in EOS?**

## Benefits

### Scalable & Fast
Industry leading speed and latency in transactions and throughput

### Cost-Effective
Flexible cost model by resources for operation with zero transaction fees

### Eco-Friendly
Sustainable and energy-efficient consensus mechanism built for performance

In blockchains like Bitcoin and Ethereum, the generation of blocks is done through a process known as *mining*. The concept of mining was introduced as a way of solving the problem of equitable distribution. During those days, the gold to be mined was in abundance. However, as more people joined the blockchain, the gold has become scarce as a result of increased mining activity. The concept of mining is now not useful since the miner who possesses the largest mining capacity is the one who owns a sophisticated mining technology or more money. The geographical distribution of the gold was very okay, and this limited the ability of any individual with sophisticated technology to control it.

Other than the above challenge, the mining concept is associated with other weaknesses. It is useless, unfair and it consumes too much electricity. Again, the process does not increase the cryptography of the network as most people think. The Proof of Work miners don't add any useful services to the network. The reason is that they incur high costs of buying mining equipment and paying for electricity.

EOS has changed completely as it doesn't require any mining to be done. It introduced the DPOS algorithm which allows voters to serve the network by voting and they are rewarded for the services they offer. Note that only services that are developed well and highly accepted by the user community because of their benefit are rewarded. This was a new invention that made many programmers spend their time while servicing the EOS network, providing professional products not available in any other blockchain network. EOS comes with a unique design and features that cannot be found in any other blockchain platform, showing that EOS is a product from an independent developer. The network was developed for free before the developer could begin to earn returns from the generation of blocks.

Of all the available cryptocurrencies, EOS has the largest number of wallets for PCs, mobile phones and web browsers. The EOS blockchain provides at least 9 tools good for network data analysis, 11 block explores for EOS network only, various sites and tools for guidance and training of developers, more than 30 channels on YouTube all dedicated towards EOS and at least 20 decentralized exchange platforms.

**Voting in EOS**
In the previous sections, we stated that EOS uses the Delegated Proof of Stake (DPOS) algorithm to help the users reach a consensus. This means that the EOS blockchain is a democratic system

similar to running of governments in which all citizens are allowed to go through a voting process instead of allowing a few individuals to make decisions on their behalf.

In EOS, the voting is done by the holders of the EOS currency holders using a recorded and authenticated operation inside the blockchain, which helps avoid any suspicion of error or fraud.

The purpose of voting in blockchains is to make important decisions regarding the network, such as selection of network operators, the block producers. The block producers represent those who voted for them in the same way that a member of parliament in a country represents his or her constituents. The greatest advantage with this is that EOS allows for changing of the vote in case the block producer makes a decision that is not in line with the expectations of the voters in terms of the future and benefit of the network. This is a great feature introduced by EOS to guarantee its users of voting credibility and validity.

However, a number of people have criticized this voting mechanism. The reason behind the criticism is the relationship between the voting weight and the number of owned EOS currencies, that is, the relative weight, not the population number. To answer this criticism, the population number should not be given the highest consideration in respect to a public property. It is similar to a company in which decisions are made by the largest shareholders, not the employees nor the little investors. An individual with high shareholding will care more about the network interest compared to a person with a minimal shareholding. A person who owns a few currencies on EOS will not care much about the future of the platform.

Note that any holder of an EOS account is allowed to launch a referendum that is related to any topic they are interested in, which means that they will enjoy the same reliability and credibility of voting on the blockchain.

## What are Proxies?

The purpose of proxies is to provide a second layer of voting, which simplifies the follow-up process followed by the EOS currency holders. The proxies relieve the currency holders from the task of having to follow up after the block producers to know the details of their works and understand their credibility and the service they add to the network.

The currency holders simply vote for the proxies and the proxies vote on their behalf to choose to select the best block producers and do away with the voting in any case the efficiency drops.

From the above discussion, it is very clear that EOS is the best blockchain network so far. This is because it combines the best technologies with the best governance models and brings them together into a one superfast platform. The blockchain has an unlimited scalability, making it good for business needs.

**How does EOS Work?**

EOS and Ethereum blockchain platforms are similar when it comes to host dApps. However, EOS is more advanced because of its ability to exceed the total number of transactions that can be processed on the platform per second, which is more than 50 thousand transactions per second.

EOS is also famous for its unlimited scalability. EOS had outperformed all other blockchain networks in terms of the number of transactions that can be handled per second even before the parallel and multithreading technologies were implemented.

EOS employs the use of "ownership model" on its network, where the ownership of the network resources is proportional or equivalent to the amount of token that one owns on the network. For example, a user who owns 2 EOS owns two of a billion of the EOS network NET, CPU resources. This is because the network has a total of 1 billion EOS tokens. This means that the user is able to own and use resources depending on the number of stakes that he owns on the network instead of having to pay for every transaction that he owns, explaining why there is no transaction fees on the platform. In addition to that, the network allows its users to maintain their shares and develop freemium apps that provide an easy access to the new by a large number of new users.

The flexibility of the network is seen in its ability to allow the users to delegate their stake usage or rent their network resources to the other developers so as to use them for development of their own dApps.

**What is EOS REX?**

EOS REX stands for EOS Resource Exchange, and it is a platform developed to be used as the central place for trading network resources (CPU, NET) and provide the dApp developers with an easy way of obtaining resources much easily and quickly. The network users are also able to rent any resource that they do not need to other users.

The EOS platform operates on the ownership model where the user is the owner of the platform not just a person paying to use the network resources. This has seen the network improve its intrinsic value.

**EOS Features**

EOS provides complete identification and authentication systems and multiple levels of permissions, by which permissions for other users or applications can be set. If an account is stolen, the recovery feature is provided.

Currently, features for cloud storage and server hosting are being developed. Such features will allow the developers to create and upload products online directly on the EOS platform.

The EOS blockchain will be capable of handling up to 1 million transactions per second in a single chain, and infinite number of transactions on multiple blockchains that have been connected to the main chain.

On EOS, no micropayments are required. On most blockchain networks, the users have to pay so as to send messages or carry out tasks on the block. In EOS, the developers are given the freedom of determining the nature of the transaction fees that is associated with their decentralized applications.

EOS has a good governance and management model, which provides the developer community with an efficient manner of developing applications and fixing any bugs in them. The model is run by block producers, who are given the authority to verify transactions that were completed during downtime, and they cannot approve it until maintenance has been done.

With EOS, performance can be optimized since the blocks are designed to be resized depending on the size of the incoming transactions.

**Daniel Larimer (BM)**

## Daniel Larimer

**CHIEF TECHNOLOGY OFFICER** | BLACKSBURG, VA

Dan is one of the leading innovators, engineers and thought leaders in the blockchain space. He is the co-founder of an array of successful blockchain companies, most notably the decentralized exchange BitShares, the social media network Steemit, and Block.one, publisher of the EOSIO protocol, all of which provide industrial- and enterprise-grade blockchain solutions utilizing the widely-adopted Delegated Proof of Stake (DPOS) consensus mechanism, which he invented. Recognized as an industry pioneer, Dan is one of the most high-profile figures in the blockchain arena, having garnered a decade's worth of entrepreneurial and technical experience in the field. At Block.one, he is the lead architect behind the EOSIO software, which is engineered to run highly scalable blockchain applications. He is an alumnus of the Virginia Tech Department of Computer Science, where he currently serves as a guest lecturer and curriculum advisor.

🐦 in M Ω

There is no doubt that EOS is a product of great intelligence. You must be asking yourself, who is behind this intelligence? This is after knowing the features and the advantages of the EOS blockchain compared to the other blockchain networks. It will be good for you to know where the idea began and how it later became a success story.

Daniel Larimer is the man behind this great blockchain platform. He is counted among the crypto pioneers and he has little experience in blockchain technology and development. He has severally discussed the scalability of Bitcoin on Bitcointalk forum and its lack of capacity to handle multiple transactions in case the world turn into using Bitcoin.

He has also successfully developed three other blockchain projects including Steem, Bitshares and EOS. His journey in the blockchain technology started in 2014 after he launched his first project, Bitshares. Bitshares received a great reception in the market due to its ability to process transactions at a high speed and for providing the first large-scale decentralized platform for carrying out trades.

Daniel also developed a blockchain technology named *Graphene*. Later, Graphene became the fastest blockchain technology implemented since the developer had employed some engineering mechanisms during its construction.

He is also the brain behind the DPOS algorithm which has widely been used by other blockchain implementations such as TRON, Nano, Lisk, Tezos, ICX and several others.

His journey of developing blockchain networks did not stop there. In 2016, he developed Steem. Steem is a blockchain platform in which writers of useful articles are paid. The writers create content in the form of articles and they are rewarded in monetary terms, in a mining-like manner. The platform has been successful and it currently has a large number of users. It clearly shows how the blockchain technology can be used to create and run successful applications and projects. Millions of users are currently earning from the platform by publishing their articles on it.

Dan has been programming since his childhood. His cultural interests made it easy for him to understand how the global economy works. He employed this into the EOS project. Dan also has interest in philosophy, mostly the game theory, and he has contributed significantly into the subject.

EOS was Dan's third project. The project attracted media attention even before it was launched. Block.One is the founder of EOS as they developed its code. The project has received much funding since its beginning from famous investors including Mike Novogratz.

The great experience of the Block.One team in the blockchain technology and computing has seen the success of the EOS project. They have a great experience in the development of blockchain applications, not forgetting that their team is made up of the best consultants, developers and investors from all over the world.

Block.One was responsible for laying the foundation of EOS, right from the first step. In 2017, they publicly announced the launch of EOS. Yes, but all of it can be attributed to Daniel Larimer. It is his creative mind that is behind everything about EOS. It is worth noting that the EOSIO platform is not managed by the Block.One but it is managed by the block producers. Currently, there are a total of 121 block producers on the platform. There is a cooperation between the Block.One company and the currency community, and this has seen the success of the project. This means that even though the company is playing a significant role in developing the project, it is receiving a lot of support from the community of block producers. The company is not the only entity behind the development of the project.

EOS can be described as a very disruptive technology in the field of development of decentralized applications, and its features are expected to change the market rules. During its crowd funding phase, the project receives a lot of funds that have made it possible for the team to hire the best brains from all over the world.

# Chapter 4- Voice

Voice is a social media platform. From its name, Voice is a social media platform on which every user will have a Voice. On the ordinary social media platforms, you need to have millions of followers for your voice to be heard. This is not the case with Voice. Instead of having followers, you can air your voice using the Voice tokens. Voice can be described as the greatest implementation in the cryptocurrency space.

Do you remember the problems we discussed previously about the ordinary social media platforms? If you have ever used any social media platform, you must have noticed that digital interactions are marked by fake followers, cyber bullies and fake followers. The users are tracked and influenced by hidden algorithms, and their thinking and behavior are influenced by those who get their personal data on their hands. Group discussions are filled with insults and hate and offensive content is not rare. Social media was made to help people exchange their thoughts and ideas, but it has turned out to be a garbage bin where people throw their dirty content. Social media users are also being used as free commodities from which profit is extracted. Every word, like, photo, picture, video and view is being monetized by the social media giants and sold for a hefty price, with the users not getting even a single cent from the earned revenue. The users are the owners of the platforms, not the company nor the advertisers.

The users of platforms such as Twitter, YouTube and Facebook have created a circle of friends, family and followers. The reason they find it difficult to leave to another platform is that they don't want to leave that circle. And in case any user is willing to move to a new platform, there is nothing new being offered in the new solution. This can be termed to be a prisoners' dilemma, but Voice is changing it.

Voice will offer a lasting solution to these problems. Voice will leverage the EOS blockchain to provide the world with the most transparent and aligned social media platform. Voice will make the users benefit from their engagements, not the companies. The social media platform will be using the VOICE token. According to Dan, the brain behind Voice, the VOICE token has the fairest distribution of tokens across the world.

The unique thing about the VOICE token is that it cannot be created by burning electricity. In the beginning, the only way to generate the token is by REAL people communicating to each other or by creating great content.( Voice can be bought on the market after the registrants release their token gaining by activity.)  As you know, some social media accounts are not of REAL or unique people. The question is, how will Voice ensure that each account is held by a unique and REAL person? This will be achieved by employing a multistep authentication process to ensure that each account is unique and that it is owned by a REAL person.

With your VOICE token, it will be possible for you to increase the visibility of your content, or even help other platform users find any content that you found to be interested. In case a user voices their comment before yours, you will get back your VOICE tokens and extra ones. Signing up for an account on the platform will be free, so no need to worry about the starting cost.

There is something else that makes Voice to be more than just a social media platform. It allows other applications that run on the EOS blockchain to create applications enabled with a unique identity. This means that application developers on the EOS platform will be able to leverage the VOICE token for their own benefit. This will change everything, making it easy for developers to build applications on the EOS platform.

A design with such a design and concept will greatly revolutionize the social media industry. Voice will introduce a fair, transparent and an equal society to all individuals.

**The Unique Identity Solution for Secure Digital Identity**

Block.One has invented a solution for ensuring that there is a secure digital identity of users on their platforms. The current solutions of ensuring a secure digital identity rely on government issued documents that are prone to forgery. The solution has introduced a model of governance that will uniquely identify individuals by minimizing the probability of a user being a fake person. Voice will be a great beneficiary of this feature. The feature was launched just few days to the release of Voice. The solution comes with methods that will address the requirements of a reliable and distributed identity solution.

Here are the ways through which the solution will provide a secure digital identity to users:

- Creation of a verifiable digital identity
- Proving that a device belongs to an individual
- Tying each user device to a private key
- Creation of a first user-generated item with an identifiable feature
- Signing the first user-generated item digitally to create a secure digital artifact.
- Uploading of the first user-generated item and the secure digital artifact to an auditable public chain
- Verification of the digital identity of a user by auditing the auditable chain
- Obtaining the generated second user-generated item with an identifiable feature.
- Comparing the first and the second user-generated items.
- Uploading the second user-generated item to a public ledger if the comparison is within the recommended threshold.

The solution will follow the workflow given below:

1. Authentication to identify the device linked to a user

   Each user's device will be authenticated and linked to the user. A multi-authentication approach will be employed to make sure that this is done correctly. Some of the authentication mechanisms to be employed include password, an audio signature and a biometric input. The biometric input will be fingerprint or facial recognition. Each user can only be in one place at a time. Each device can also be only in one place at a time. The location of both the user and the device will be used to create a digital identity an avoid forgery. As a user takes photos of themselves, their digital identity associated with the device will become more established and secure.

2. Creation of a verifiable digital identity

   A memory will be used to store a sequence of instructions. A processor will also be provided to execute these instructions to verify the device and its ownership. The execution of the instructions will also make the processor tie the device to a private key that is located on the device. The processor will also obtain the first user-generated item that was generated through the device, which has an identifiable feature of the user.

3. Generation of a secured digital artifact and uploading it to an auditable public chain

   The processor will sign the user-generated item to create a secure digital identity artifact. The generated secure digital identity artifact will be uploaded to an auditable chain of public ledger. The second user-generated item will have the identifiable feature of the user. The two, the first user-generated item and the second user-generated item will be hashed together to create a link on the auditable chain. The first and the second user-generated items will have live photographs of not less than two distinct users that have been generated through the device.

4. Verifying the user's digital identity

   The digital identity of the user will be verified by auditing the auditable chain. The verification of the first user-generated item is done by verifying the identifiable feature, the private key, the signature and link to the device. The verification of the second user-generated item is done by comparing the identifiable feature of the user obtained from the first user-generated user item to that obtained from the second user-generated item.

**Decentralized Finance on EOSIO**

DeFi (Decentralized Finance) is simply a shared community of modular frameworks or open-source protocols used for creating and issuing digital assets. Some of its products include security tokens, lending protocols, exchanges, derivatives, prediction markets and others.

According to Daniel Larimer, Ethereum didn't succeed in DeFi (Decentralized Finance). DeFi refers to conventional financial tools that are built on the blockchain, specifically Ethereum. The on-chain transactions that run on the Ethereum ledger lead to high wait time and transaction fees, which are not applicable to an order book and they may lead to inaccuracy. Ethereum has a low performance such that the wait times is in the form of minutes, and this causes a mismatch in timing between the submission of an order by a marker and the fulfillment of an order by a taker. This explains why most decentralized exchanges running on Ethereum use off-chain order books. Examples include 0x, EtherDelta, AirSwap, and IDEX.

This is also the reason as to why Bancor does not use an order book but it instead uses liquidity reserves. Bancor stores toke reserves that can be exchanged by anyone who wishes to exchange tokens and the pricing is calculated using a formula that takes into consideration the reserve supply of every token plus the constant reserve ratio.

EOSIO provides a simpler decentralized finance system since the wait time is in terms of milliseconds and no transaction fees is charged. The performance of EOSIO permits the use of an on-chain order book kept directly on the distribution ledger. This way, all orders can be submitted to the distribution ledger network and then be confirmed by the network.

On EOSIO, anyone is allowed to host and access the copy of order book, and anyone can submit orders to be added to the order book. EOSIO was developed on the grapheme technology, just as Bitshares, which was the first decentralized cryptocurrency exchange developed by Daniel Larimer. EOS marks the blockchain with the highest user activity and other EOSIO are ranked at the top.

**Accountability in Voice**

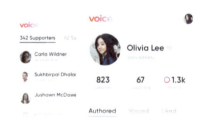

Before the invention of the internet, the sharing of news was controlled by television networks, newspapers and large publishers. After the introduction of the internet in the 1900s and 2000s, giant social media platforms such as Facebook were discovered. Today, Facebook owns the four leading social media platforms in the world. Even though Facebook doesn't generate or produce news, it greatly controls how this news is shared worldwide.

In 2019, Facebook deleted more than 2 billion fake accounts. However, nothing was done to solve the problem of Facebook selling its user data to the highest bidder.

Recently, Facebook announced how they intend to moderate content on their platform, and this revelation is very frightening, and even the worst approach. They are planning to move the surveillance and censorship from their servers to the users' mobile phones. This means that content moderation will be done directly on the user devices. This means that Facebook will be able to delete a message on your device if it violates its rules even before you can send it. Facebook has also stated that when a user installs their Facebook app on his or her mobile phone, the user grants them the legal right to track the user's real time location, phone microphone, camera and even the non-uploaded photos that are on the phone. Such kind of surveillance on users is not good.

The solution to this problem is to connect real people to real people, not hidden trolls and bots and having people take responsibility of what they post and share. This will eliminate the need of us having to censor and surveil our public discourse. The world is full of fake news, and it's important for us to know the source of any news. People need to differentiate between fake and real news, and this explains the importance of establishing identity in social media platforms. It's always easy to spread fake news or content with poor quality if the process is being done by bots who share and upvote, but if the user is a uniquely identified person, the cyber bullies or bots will not find any place on the platforms.

The solution to this is building accountability on the social media platform. With the current social media platforms, it is possible for a person or a group of persons to create hundreds of thousands of fake accounts, fake likes, fake posts, fake everything. This is chaotic and a hindrance to reality and illusion. You as a real person are not in need of faking your identity or story.

To solve these problems, there is a need to develop a social media platform that runs on a decentralized blockchain in which the identities and sources of the sources of posted content may be proved, without providing the personal data of users to individuals with selfish interests like advertisers. The outcome of this will be Real voices from Real people creating Real content, Real value and Real attention.

Block.One saw this opportunity and developed Voice, a decentralized social media application, platform and token. Voice has created a revolutionary response to the invasive social media model of censorship and surveillance. The reason is that it will not sell your personal data to advertisers and return the multi-billion dollar social media ad revenue stream back to the rightful owner, who is YOU, the content creator and the commenter. Voice has turned the entire social media model upside-down, inside-out so as to benefit the individuals who make it, like YOU.

The use of a special authentication system on Voice will make sure that there are no fake accounts on the network. This will also help do away with catfishes, robots and burner accounts. The Voice token will introduce a level playing field. Daniel Larimer describes it as the fairest crypto token since it can only be generated or created via real digital interactions. During the identity check conducted on the individuals joining the network, a government-provided ID will be required. This will help to minimize spam.

In Voice, there are similar rules for everyone, the platform, the user and the contributor, and there are no invisible interests, hidden algorithms, but just a game field in which everyone is given equal chances to be heard.

**How Voice Works**

## Now the fun part.

Your post goes live! When other users like it, you earn Voice tokens and your post gains visibility. The more popular your post — the more you earn.

In Voice, every user will have to sign up by going through a thorough authentication system to make sure that they are a real person. The information provided for authentication process will be kept private. Your account profile will only show your first name, your last name and your country of residence. Voice, unlike other social media platforms, will not sell your data to advertisers. Identity verification is key in social media since a real individual will care much about their own reputation. On the other hand, an individual running a fake social media account will have nothing to lose by pushing hidden agendas or fake content. Voice will change this by providing at least one place for civil public disclosure.

The goal of most social media platforms is to get your personal data and auction it to the highest bidder, who will in turn flood your feeds with hidden agendas. That is why Block.One has created Voice, a social media platform that is more aligned with the world by promoting and cultivating proper content creation, curation and sharing. Voice will be a self-sustaining platform of ideas, where the users will benefit directly from their ideas and engagement on the platform.

After signing up for a Voice account, all users are given an equal number of Voice tokens. After that, the users will get a Universal Basic Income (UBI) each day. If you want more people to see your tokens, you can use Voice tokens to promote them. If people like your Voice posts, you will be paid some Voice tokens, and these will have value. The re for this value is that advertisers will need to purchase Voice tokens so as to place and run ads.

As a user, you can sell your Voice tokens or use them to promote your Voice posts. However, even if you sell your Voice tokens, you will get additional ones the next day. This means that you will continuously have voice tokens, and your task will be to choose what you need to do with the tokens.

In Voice, all functions will be made transparent, meaning that transparency will become the core of the EOS blockchain. By this, it means that there will be no algorithms to determine your feeds, nor will there be invisible hands that manipulate the way users think and interact with each other on the platform. All voice smart contracts will EOS so as to run. Currently, EOS forms the largest blockchain in the world. 60.6% of blockchain users prefer EOS blockchain. 48% of daily active blockchain users use EOS. For a transaction to be completed, a cpu/net will be required and the state of the app will be maintained by a RAM.

In Steem, which is a social media platform developed Dan Larimer, users noticed a great weakness in that the rich get more power on the platform compared to the other users. When developing Voice, this was put into consideration. In Voice, your power will come from the ability to great high quality content but not from the fact that you are wealthy. The Voice platform will also operate on the basis of one man one vote.

Dan Larimer, being good in game theory, employed this technique when developing Voice. The game theory is very powerful. See every post on Voice as a pixel on a pixel master. After finding a good content, you voice it, that is, you like it. As long as you are not the last user to voice or like the post, you will earn some Voice tokens. If you become the last person to voice the content, you content will be more visible and it will have high chances of earning likes.

The users will be able to transfer Voice tokens between each other. Remember that the users will not Voice tokens by buying them. However, the transfer of tokens between the users will be done or regulated by jurisdictions. This will help prevent a scenario of having some users buy votes. The Voice users will be able to use their Voice identity to sign up for accounts on other dapps. A way of dealing with offensive content will be introduced in Voice. In such a case, the user will be bumped down. If there is censorship, the user will be paid. This means that if any user wants to get out of Voice, they will get back their tokens.

**The VOICE Token**

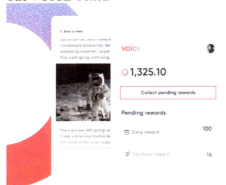

## Raise your Voice.

So you've earned some Voice tokens, what can you do with them? After making a comment — Voice it! Use your tokens to put your opinion on top and ensure your Voice is heard. If someone else raises their Voice above yours, you get your tokens back plus some extra Voice.

Currently, most of the available social media platforms are available for free. You can use social media platforms such as Twitter, Facebook and Instagram without incurring any economic cost. However, the recent scandals have clearly shown that these social media platforms are monetizing you, your media, information and online habits. If you are not paying for a product, then you are the product. The social media platforms where created to use their users, so it's the companies that are reaping rewards, not the users.

With the blockchain technologies and crypto assets, this issue can be turned on its head, and the consumers will be able to gain control over their information. Bloc.One has discovered Voice to empower social media users and change the way things are done in social media platforms. Voice will provide the world with a more transparent social media platform by promoting good content and reward the creators of such content.

Voice will revolutionize the social media platforms by introducing transparency, security of accounts, accountability and the absence of hidden interests and algorithms. It will be possible to create the Voice token for empowering and rewarding users for every piece of content that they create as well as for their interactions. This means that the Voice token will form the foundation by which interactions are done on the platform. The platform will definitely become a home for great content.

The token will be used for rewarding unique users content creation, content discovery and empower their voices. Your rewards will be determined by how much people like your posts or your comments on other posts. This is a new and unique feature since on social media platforms like Facebook, Instagram and Twitter, each like on a post generates revenue for companies. On Voice, this will be different as each user will be rewarded for the content they create and for the other users' engagement with the post. This is greatly beneficial and its importance should not be underestimated.

Users will earn Voice tokens for posting their content. If they want other platform users to hear their voice, which will give smaller users an opportunity to others hear their voice.

Other than the economic rewards associated with the token, your post will gain visibility, meaning each interaction will fuel your post. Voice operates under a simple mechanism: post your content, get rewards from comments and likes which will increase the visibility of post, bring more likes and followers to your post. Just "voice it" to attract more visibility and engagement.

Block.One, the company behind Voice, has introduced a way of boosting your content, "voicing" or "voice it". It will be possible for you to use the rewards that you earn so as to voice your posts and comments so as to make them more visible and attract more attention to them. With this mechanism, you will stay on the top and when another user voices their comment to bring your comment down, you will get back your tokens and an additional 10% tokens as a reward. The Voice it feature will earn you rewards by 30% if another user pays more than you. The user who has out-voiced you will not take the rewards but they get more likes and visibility for their content.

The introduction of the Voice token does not mean that the EOS token will lose its value or purpose. Although the Voice token will be used to voice content, it will not be usable for allocating cpu/net/ram. This is what the EOS token will be used for, meaning that its use case is not be lost.

# How Voice Rewards its Users

## Claim your Voice.

Everyone gets some Voice just for showing up. This means everyone has a chance to be heard. What do *you* want to Voice?

Voice will revolutionize the way people interact with the digital world and reward its users for every content that they share instead of being used by companies to steal personal data of its users and feed their hidden algorithms. Good content will be given priority and rewards for creating such content will go back to the user and the community. The aim of Voice is to introduce a self-sustaining economy of thoughts and ideas since what is good for the platform is also good for the users. On Voice, the focus will put on users, since they are the ones accountable for whatever content they share.

Today, Facebook has more than 2 billion active users. These users have joined the platform to connect with their relatives, friends and do business. However, whenever ay company grows too big, things get out of hand leading to poor client satisfaction. Yes, Facebook is the largest social media platform in the world, but it is only ranked at position 7 in terms of user satisfaction. The platform is outpaced by other social media platforms such as Wikipedia, YouTube and Pinterest. Facebook is the leading platform and app in terms of visits, but this is not in proportion to the customer satisfaction.

When a user likes your Voice post, you earn Voice tokens. When you comment on another user's post and other users like your comment, you earn Voice tokens. This shows that people will be seeking attention so as to earn. Don't forget that when you Voice (like) a post, you will be helping other users to find the content that they might like. This process is happening in the current social media platforms, but users don't earn anything from it.

For a user to promote his or her comment, they are required to have some amount of tokens. For the next user to promote their comment to the top spot, they will be required to pay tokens that are 15% more than those paid by the original content promoter, meaning that the original promoter will have earned profit. In addition to this, another 15% will have to be paid to the user who actually created the post that is being commented on, and the user will have also made profit. The user who is promoting their comment will pay a total 30% premium above the last comment promoter plus the original amount. This comment will comment for the next 24 hours after the last like.

The rewards will not depend on the number of tokens that you own. They depend on your identity. The platform brings transparency to the paid influence. On ordinary social media platforms like Facebook, advertisers pump USDs into their accounts to run ads, and the profits go to only a few shareholders, while the users earn nothing. The voice token provides a mechanism to decentralize the control amongst the user of the platform and give all of them an equal chance of taking part in the influence.

Most people come to social media to seek attention. Only a limited amount of attention is provided to the users. There is a demand to see content and demand to promote content. A means of managing the demand and supply is needed. This is the means that is used for interaction on the Voice community. It's now possible to stay civilized on social media. If you create a good content that other people enjoy hearing, you will have the opportunity of having your voice heard by other people and this will be mediated by the Voice token.

Voice is not a platform for sharing and liking content only. Block.One added the Universal Basic Income (UBI) feature that we mentioned previously, with which users will be given Voice tokens each day just for using the platform. The good thing with the UBI feature is that it will make it impossible for influencers to maintain their influence by just holding tokens since the tokens will be burned when they voice their content. This will provide an opportunity for the new users to have some level of influence on the platform. Exchanging control for visibility is a great feature that will encourage the platform users to use their tokens to voice their content.

According to Brendan Blumer, the CEO of Block.One, the top influencers on Voice will be able to earn between $50 and $100 million as revenue from the platform. The top influencers who can bring 50 million followers to the network will be able to make tens, or hundreds of thousands of dollars and redefine their net worth. The marketing efforts on the platform will be geared towards bringing such influencers to the network. The network will be sustained by good content from the users, but the network won't be sustained by corporates.

Since Voice will run on the EOS blockchain, the content posted by users on Voice will be recorded publicly on the blockchain. The network will leverage the Voice token to reward the content creators and allow them to promote their content. Voice users will not be allowed to purchase or mine the Voice token directly, but they will be issued an amount of Voice tokens each day which they can use to promote their content.

You may agree or disagree with the fact that Voice will be issuing its users with an airdrop of Voice tokens each day, but this is a clear indication that Voice is interested in attracting users who believe that they can use their content creation skills as a source of income, especially on social media platforms. However, the company behind the platform, Block.One, has not stated how they will benefit from the Voice network.

Blumer, the CEO of Block.One has predicted that there Voice will have users who will gather up to hundred million of followers. Even top influencers such as Katy Perry and Miley Cyrus have not amassed that amount of following. On Steemit, which is social media platform developed by Daniel Larimer, the top influencers have only managed to amass tens of thousands of followers. IF Voice follows the approach employed by Steemit, there will be such influencers. After the launch of Steemit in 2016, the platform attracted content creators by featuring wealthy users capable of generating sustainable income by investing in the tokens of the platform. Steemit had promised to improve content curation by rewarding the users who post and curate content by use of a set of tokens. Steemit attracted from the community of cryptocurrency users but it did not generate a widespread appeal. The question is, will Voice succeed in the area where Steemit has failed? There is no doubt that Voice will take the digital world by a storm. The $150 invested in the project shows that Block.One takes it with serious and their team is dedicated to see the project succeed.

Note that it will be free for the users to post a post or a comment. When you boost the post or comment, you will burn a percentage of Voice tokens, a percentage will be paid to the owner of the top comment and a percentage will be paid to the owner of the post.

**Advertising on Voice**

Voice will also introduce a new way of advertising, something that has never been seen before. There will be no flashy banners and nobody will be allowed to buy huge sums of tokens to boost their posts so that they can stay at the top and in a visible position. Every user will have an equal opportunity of being heard, but Voice will change the ability to sell or transfer this right. If a user needs to cede their own voice power to another user, they will be able to do so at a price. This means that the advertisers will buy the tokens and they will be burned.

Your choice will be determined by what you value, which can be your own voice or the revenue that you will earn from it. This shows that Voice has the potential of becoming the first place for user-generated revenue on social media.

The businesses will have their voice on the platform, but they will not have similar privileges as other individuals. Their likes won't increase rewards and they won't get UBI, meaning that individual users will have more of an edge than companies, preventing the possibility of having the system compromised by businesses to have their agendas passed. Businesses will be allowed to use their Voice tokens so as to voice their content.

With such a unique identity and reward system in place, Voice has all it takes to take the digital world by a storm. It will be a platform where content and comments of a high quality will gain a high visibility and bullies will not be accepted. Social media has shaped the current society of garbage posts and short attention spans, and in the same way, Voice will turn things around and add value to creators of high quality content.

This means that Voice tokens will be the key to marketing on the platform. If you are a marketer, it will be easy for you, just buy Voice tokens, create your content, post it and use the Voice tokens to voice it. It is after this that your content will be able to reach as many people as possible. The advertisers will be allowed to buy advertisements by use of Voice tokens that could have been burned.

# Chapter 5- Conclusion

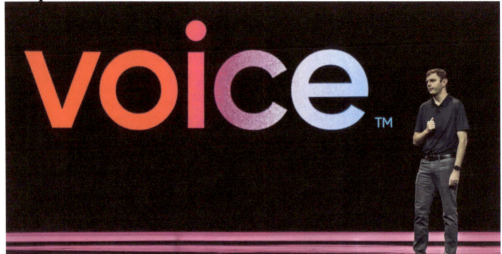

There is an increasing use of social media platforms all over the world. Nearly each person has 1 or 2 social media accounts. These people use social media platforms as a way of connecting with their friends, relatives and acquaintances. The rise in the popularity of social media networks can be attributed to the invention of the internet. The internet has changed the way things are done, even interacting with one another.

Social media users only see the social media networks as a platform for them to use for their interactions. However, with the recent scandals, it is very clear that this is not the case. There are a number of challenges that need to be addressed with social media platforms. What users don't know is that they are the owners of the social media networks, not the companies or developers. However, the companies have not put this into consideration. Although the users are the real owners of the platforms, they don't earn any profits from the networks, but only a few self-centered individuals take home profits.

One of the problems with social media platforms is accountability and user identity. It is not hard for you to create tens or even hundreds of fake accounts on social media platforms. With a fake account, one can post the kind of content they want since they don't care about their reputation. If you opened the account using fake details, you will not care about the kind of content that you post on the platform.

The privacy of personal user data has also become a challenge on social media platforms. People are giving out their personal details when signing up for social media accounts. They are asked to provide details such as their names, the dates of birth, country of origin, gender etc. This is a lot of information and it has ended up being misused to benefit a few individuals instead of the owners of the information. Social media platforms are selling the private information of their users to the highest bidder. That is why you see hundreds of ads each day when browsing on the networks. These ads are run by bots and hidden algorithms.

Most social media platforms have developed mobile apps for their networks. Users install these apps on their mobile devices without knowing what happens in the background. These apps are able to use the geo-location features of your mobile device to track your location in real time. Again, when you check in your locations, they are able to know the malls that you visit, the cities you tour etc. This is dangerous, even for your personal safety. The apps can access your device camera and even the storages.

To solve all the above problems, Block.One has invented Voice, a social media platform that will run on the EOS blockchain. Voice has been developed with the user in mind. The team behind the network considered the fact that the users are the owners of the platform, not the company. That is why the benefits earned on the platform will go back to the real owner, the user, not the company. They have introduced a way for people to earn for their engagement on social media. This means that your stay on social media will not be benefitting someone else, but you.

On Voice, the identity of users will be taken seriously so as to avoid the case of having fake accounts. Each user will go through a series of authentication steps to ensure that they are who they claim to be. A government issued id will also be required for one to join the Voice network.

The goal behind Voice is to promote the creation of good content. If you create a good content, other users on the platform will engage it, and you will earn from it. Content will be engaged through likes (voice it) and comments. Note that only few personal details will be shown your profile.

The Voice platform will be run by the Voice token. When you sign up for an account, you will be assigned some Voice tokens. This is universal to all users. However, as you engage the content of other users, your Voice tokens will be burned. The Voice tokens cannot be generated through mining. Instead, each user will be assigned a number of Voice tokens each day through the initiative of UBI. It will be possible for users to transfer Voice tokens to each other, but this will be under some jurisdictions.

The goal of any advertiser is to reach as many users as possible. Voice has made this possible. However, this will not be done using bots and hidden algorithms. The advertiser will have to use Voice tokens to voice their content so that it can reach many users. Everything will be posted publicly on the EOS blockchain.

Note that the Voice token will not eliminate the use case of the EOS token. The Voice token will be used for voicing content on the platform, but the EOS token will be used to assign cpu/net/ram to the users.

# Image Source

https://voice.com/blog/road-to-beta/

https://cfcnews.com/172238

http://tech.sina.com.cn/csj/2017-12-06/doc-ifypikwu1707122.shtml

https://block.one/events/#gallery-18

https://block.one/events/#gallery-19

https://block.one/team/dan-larimer/

https://block.one/events/#gallery-27

https://eos.io/build-on-eosio/

https://eos.io/news/analysis-of-bancor-equations-supporting-rex/

www.ingramcontent.com/pod-product-compliance
Lightning Source LLC
Chambersburg PA
CBHW041155050326
40690CB00004B/571